*our wonderful*
**weather**

valerie bodden

# snow

creative 🍎 education

*our wonderful*
**weather**

Published by Creative Education
P.O. Box 227, Mankato, Minnesota 56002
Creative Education is an imprint of The Creative Company
www.thecreativecompany.us

Design and production by Christine Vanderbeek
Art direction by Rita Marshall
Printed by Corporate Graphics in the United States of America

Photographs by Alamy (J Marshall-Tribaleye Images), Corbis (Bettmann, Ed Darack/Science
Faction, Jim Reed Photography, Frans Lanting, Eric Nguyen, Bill Stevenson/Aurora Photos, Michael
S. Yamashita), Dreamstime (Greg Blomberg, Brian Finestone, Michael Iwasaki), Getty Images (Per
Breiehagen, Rebecca Emery, Katherine Frey/The Washington Post, Mitchell Funk, David W. Hamilton,
Johner, Ben Klaus, Michael Melford, Steve Taylor, Bill Turnbull/NY Daily News Archive), iStockphoto
(James Boulette, Maxim Bolotnikov, Glenn Culbertson, Franky De Meyer, Matthew Dula, Evelin Elmest,
Bill Grove, Cristian Andrei Matei, Oks_Mit, VM)

Library of Congress Cataloging-in-Publication Data

Bodden, Valerie.
Snow / by Valerie Bodden.
Summary: A simple exploration of snow, examining how these icy flakes of precipitation
develop, the ways in which snow can be used and enjoyed, and the problems snow can cause.
Includes bibliographical references and index.
ISBN 978-1-60818-148-3
1. Snow—Juvenile literature. I. Title.
QC926.37.B63 2012
551.57'84—dc22    2010052763

CPSIA: 030111 PO1449

First edition
2 4 6 8 9 7 5 3 1

# contents

Snow is a form of water that falls to the ground as white flakes. Snow forms when water turns into water vapor and rises into the sky. As the water vapor gets higher, it gets colder.

The highest parts of tall mountains always have snow

water vapor

Water vapor high in the sky turns into ice crystals that form a cloud. Sometimes the ice crystals stick together.

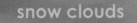

snow clouds

They form snowflakes! The wind blows clouds full of snowflakes across the sky.

Every snowflake is different.
But all snowflakes have six sides.
Snowflakes can be shaped like
plates, tubes, or stars.

Most snowflakes are less than
half an inch (1.3 cm) across

Some snowflakes are made up of only two ice crystals. But other snowflakes have more than 200 ice crystals. These big flakes can be an inch (2.5 cm) wide!

Ice crystals that build up on tree branches are called frost

Sometimes, only a little bit of snow falls. But during a cold and windy snowstorm called a blizzard, many feet of snow can fall at a time. Blizzards can drop snow over a huge area.

This house and street were buried in snow by a blizzard

Meteorologists (mee-tee-uh-RAH-luh-jists) are people who study weather. They try to forecast how the weather will change.

radar

They use radar and satellites to figure out where it
might snow. Afterward, they use a ruler to measure
how much snow has fallen.

satellite

In January 1888, a snowstorm called the Children's Blizzard hit the area that is now North and South Dakota. Hundreds of people died. In 1993, the "Blizzard of the Century" dumped up to six feet (1.8 m) of snow on the eastern part of the United States and Canada. Winds whipped at more than 100 miles (161 km) per hour. About 300 people died.

The "Blizzard of the Century" in 1993 hit big cities such as New York

Blizzards can make it dangerous to travel. It is hard to see through the snow.

snow travel

Sometimes airports have to close during a blizzard. Heavy snowfalls can knock down power lines, too.

downed power lines

Some people live where it never snows. Other people have to learn to deal with snow. They need to be careful driving in the snow. But if they dress in warm clothes, snow can be fun. All those little, white snowflakes can make a big, white snowman!

# FORMS OF WATER

Water can be in three different forms—ice, liquid, and vapor. To see this, place six ice cubes in a bowl. Leave the bowl on a table for a few hours until the ice cubes melt into water. Then place the bowl of water near a sunny window. In a few days, all the water will be gone! It will have turned into water vapor.

# GLOSSARY

century — 100 years, such as the time from the year 1900 to the year 2000

forecast — to try to figure out what is going to happen in the future, such as during the next day or week

ice crystals — small pieces of ice that have six sides and make snowflakes when they join together

power lines — wires that hang from tall poles and carry electricity to homes and other buildings

radar — a system that uses radio waves and computers to measure how far away something (such as a cloud or thunderstorm) is and how fast it is moving

satellites — machines that circle Earth in space; weather satellites can take pictures of clouds and measure temperatures

water vapor — water that has turned into drops so tiny that it rises into the air and becomes invisible

# READ MORE

Harris, Caroline. *Science Kids: Weather*. London: Kingfisher, 2009.

Helget, Nicole. *Snow*. Mankato, Minn.: Creative Education, 2007.

# WEB SITES

FEMA for Kids: Winter Storms

http://www.fema.gov/kids/wntstrm.htm
Learn more about how to stay safe during a winter storm.

Snowflake and Snow Crystal Photographs

http://www.its.caltech.edu/~atomic/snowcrystals/photos/
photos.htm
Check out close-up pictures of snowflakes.

# INDEX